GRANNY'S OLE WIVES' TALES FOLK SAYINGS And SUPERSTITIONS

Written By:

SHIRLEY A. WARREN

With Special Help From:

J.D. Mackler
William M. Nix

This Book is dedicated to:

Mom and Dad

With Special Thanks To:
My Family

Illustrations By
Sharon Nester

Copyright © 1987, 2006 by Shirley A. Warren

ISBN 978-1-4303-0399-2

All rights reserved. This work may not be used or reproduced without written permission from the author, with the exception of brief quotations used in critical review.

Additional copies may be obtained at www.lulu.com

PREFACE

Granny is a part of me and a part of many others who lived in the Deep South some 50 years ago or more. Her ancestors were of Scottish & English Descent.

She is "overindulged" with superstitions and folktales.

This book is a compilation of 'sayings' and tales I have heard over the years. Most of them actually came from my Mother and Grandmother; and are now being retold through Granny.

Many of these sayings are commonly known, but may vary with the exact phrasing or meanings.

INTRODUCTION

Come with me on an imaginary journey into the colorful world of the 'Old South' when the pace was slower and times were less complicated.

Imagine yourself walking down a dusty country road on a brisk autumn Sunday afternoon. We're going to visit Granny and chat a while and catch up on the latest gossip.

I must warn you though, Granny is a little eccentric. Don't get me wrong, she is "sharp as a tack", but she lives alone in a little three-room house way back in the country.

She is quite well known around these parts and people are always seeking her advice on everything from medicinal remedies to marriage and politics. Although a bit mysterious, she is really sweet as can be. She has an opinion on every subject; however, being superstitious by nature, she especially likes to talk about old sayings and superstitions. Once she starts talking on these topics, you may as well plan to stay a while.

Hurry up now! Her house is just past the next hollow; and I can already smell something good cooking on her wood stove.

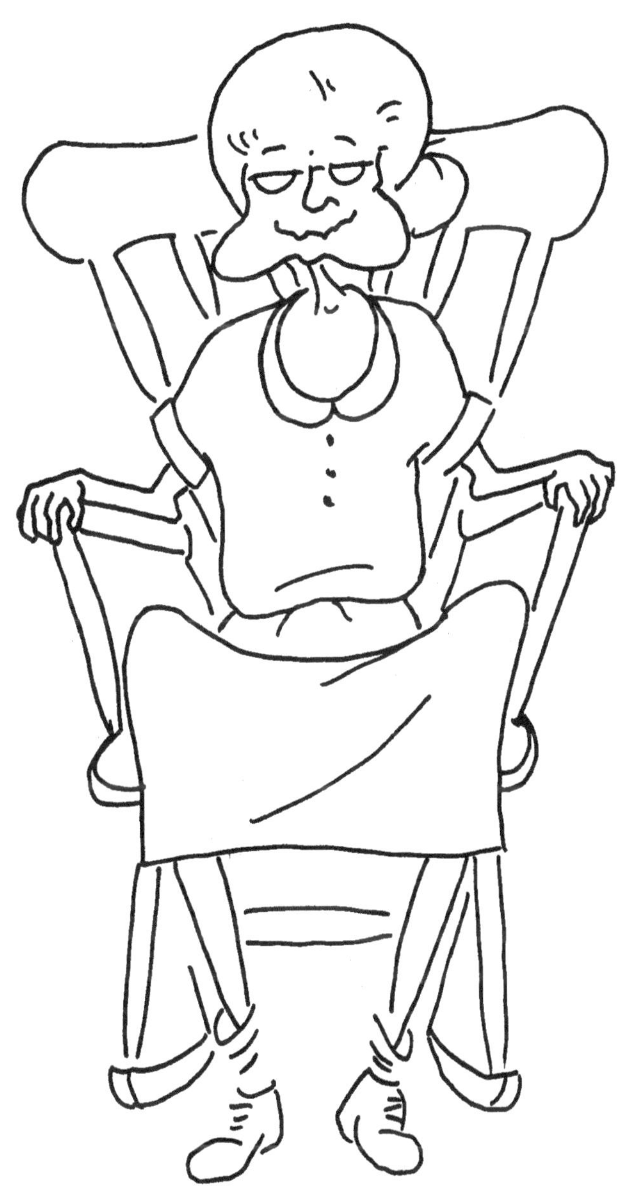

Well hello 'thar', come in and 'set' a spell. You can call me Granny; 'ever body' else does.

It's awful nice that 'yall' could come by and visit a spell.

Well, don't 'jest stand thar', come on in and 'set' 'yursef' down, and I'll call 'fer' Sally 'ta warsh' up and join us 'fer' some blackberry cobbler. Don't that sound good?

Sally is my Grand 'Yungin'. She's a 'visitin' me today and is outside 'playin'. Sally, 'hunny' what' ye' got in 'yur' hands? Don't 'ye' know if 'ye' play with frogs, 'ye'll git' warts.

Well, maybe I 'kin git' rid of them warts. My Mama always wrapped bacon 'round' my warts, and then buried the bacon; and then in a couple 'a' weeks, 'them warts was gone'.

Child, hurry and 'git' washed
up 'soes' we 'kin' set the table
and have some of that cobbler.

Now don't eat too much, cause
them blackberries can give 'ye
appendercitis'... it's the tiny seeds
'ye' know.

We 'jest' might as well go ahead and eat supper early 'soes' we 'kin' visit a spell.

Somebody must be 'comin' here hungrier than a bear cause I 'jest' put 2 spoons in this here plate.

that reminds me. . .

Did 'ye' know that if 'ye' drop a fork, that means a 'womern' is 'comin' from the 'durection' the prongs of the fork is 'pointin'.

and

If 'ye' drop a knife, a man is 'comin' from the 'durection' the blade is 'pointin'.

Do' ye wanna' pull this 'pullet' bone (wishbone) with me, 'hunny'? Whichever one of us 'gits' the longest bone 'gits ta' make a wish.

Child, did 'ye' spill that salt? 'If'n ye' did, 'ye'd' better throw some 'backards' over 'yur' left shoulder.

Lordy mercy, I dropped a dish rag. Some body is 'comin' dirtier 'n' we are.

This morning I 'fergot' my purse and didn't even remember it til I was nearly at Church. I didn't go back 'fer' it cause it's bad luck 'ta' double back. 'If'n ye fergit somethen', let it be and go 'bout' yur bizzness'.

Hee-hee! It worked out good 'fer' me, cause I had a good excuse 'fer' not 'puttin nothen' in that collection plate.

On my way back from church today, a black cat crossed my path. I didn't have a hat 'ta' turn 'round backards' to reverse the spell, so I took a 'differn't' way home.

It was a lot longer, but I don't need no more bad luck!

Good gracious alive! Look out the 'winder'. It's a 'pourin' down. . . 'rainin' cats and dogs!!!!

**It's a 'comin' up a cloud. We best head 'fer' the storm cellar.*

'Git' that dad-blamed dog away from here, he might draw lightening.

(*This means a storm is coming.)

By the way, 'ye' know if it rains when the sun's 'a shinin', it'll rain same time 'tamar' (tomorrow).

And some folks say the devil is 'beaten' his wife. But we don't have ta worry 'bout' that today; he's probably in his storm cellar too!

It's 'pecuyer' weather we're 'gittin' this time a year.

Looks like we're gonna be here 'fer' a spell.

Oh well, now's a good time 'fer' me 'ta tell ye bout' some strange 'goins' on round this neck of the woods.

FOR SALE

'Thar' was a 'womern' who lived in that ole house several years ago who told me of a strange 'happenen'.

She said that one night she was in bed, a cat jumped up on the foot of her bed. She slapped at it and her hand went right through that cat.

Now, I 'reckin' you've probably heard a lot of stories and strange tales during 'yur' lifetime; And I figure ye'lI hear a lot more. . . .

But

If 'Ye'll jest set' back and listen, this 'ole lady kin tell ye some tales' like 'ye' ain't never heard before. . . .

Did 'ya' see that ole house over yonder a mile 'er' so down the road? Well 'thar's' some stories I could tell 'ye bout' that place that'll make 'yur' hair stand on end. . .

They say a 'feller' was murdered in that house years ago, and to this day his blood stain is still on the floor. The 'floorin' has been replaced many times over the years, but the stain keeps reappearing. People say that's 'mad' blood. He's mad 'cause' they never caught the 'varmit' that murdered him. They say that 'if'n ye' walk by that ole house on a moonless night, 'ye' can still hear that poor man 'walkin' the squeaky floors!

A long time ago, when I was much younger, I 'recollect seeing somethen' that I can't explain. It was night time and I could not sleep, so I was 'jest a layin' in bed wide awake. I watched a ball of 'far' (fire) come down the stairs, go through the 'livin' room and out the 'winder'. Scared the pants off of me!

'Wher'ed' this happen 'ye' say? Why at the very house we've been 'talkin bout'.

'Ye' guessed it. I also used to live in that ole house. I'd much rather look at it from a distance and wonder 'bout' it's mysteries, than still be 'livin thar' 'wondern' if I'm 'goin' crazy.

Well, enough of 'them' spooky stories; it's a 'clearin' up now. Don't that fresh air smell good?

Let's all 'set' on the front porch and 'git' comfortable 'cause' I've got a bunch a 'sayins fer ye'.

Apple a day keeps the doctor away!

Marry a man with a lot of long hair on his *arms 'fer' he will be rich... or a good hog raiser.*

'Jest yur' luck!

'Steppin' over a grave is bad luck, so 'if'n ye' do, make sure 'ye' step 'backards' over it again!

Garlic worn 'round yur' neck will keep evil away..... 'course' it will keep 'everbody' else away too!

If'n' a turtle bites 'ye', it will not turn loose til it thunders.

Now, I know 'yall' have all been told that 'ta' open 'yur umbreller' inside the house is bad luck.

What 'ye' do on New Year's Day is what 'ye' will do all year long.

On New Year's Day, be sure to eat plenty of collard greens and black-eyed peas so that 'ye'll' have money all year long. The collard greens is 'fer' green-back money (like dollar bills) and the black-eyed peas is 'fer' coins.

When 'ye' hear a bunch of crickets 'singin' loud, that's a sign of rain.

The best 'thang fer' a bee sting is a 'gob' of snuff.

Well, it 'shore' was nice having 'yall's' company, but I got a 'heap o' chores 'ta' do before the sun sets. Why don't 'cha' come on back when 'ye' can and we'll have a good ole time telling more tales and swapping stories.

Bye now! Don't 'fergit' I'm 'jest' a 'holler' away.

MORE WISDOM FROM GRANNY

These Things Will Bring Good Luck:

Finding a penny with heads up.

Finding a 4-leaf clover.

Carrying a rabbits foot.

Finding a horseshoe and picking it up with both ends pointing upward.

Rubbing a bald man's head.

These Things Will Bring Bad Luck

A 2-dollar bill is unlucky unless you tear off one corner.

Breaking a mirror is 7 years bad luck.

Killing a robin.

Finding a penny on tails & picking it up.

Giving someone a purse or wallet without money inside.

Killing a cricket.

Picking up a horseshoe that you found with prongs pointing downward. It pours out the good luck.

Cutting bread — It must be broken.

To wear a birthstone that is not your birthstone.

To walk with one shoe on, one shoe off or to walk with someone's crutches when you do not need them.

Other Superstitions:

When the palm of your hands itch, you will have some money soon.

When the bottom of your feet itch, you will walk on strange ground.

If your right eye itches, you will be pleased.

If your left eye itches, you will be angry.

If your ears are burning, someone is talking about you.

To have very small ears means one is stingy.

A red bird in your yard means you will have company.

Never tell a nightmare before breakfast or it will come true.

If you see a shooting star, make a wish before it disappears and it will come true.

If you kill a rattlesnake and hang it over a fence or tree branch, it will rain.

If you say something boastfully, knock on wood, that the opposite does not happen.

Find a Penny — Lose a Twenty

Beer before liquor, couldn't be sicker.

Liquor before beer, have no fear.

Don't ever make fun of a child who is different, or you will have one just like it.

If a pregnant lady cuts your hair, it will grow twice as fast.

The more moles you have, the more money you will have.

Cold hands, warm heart.

If you tickle a baby's feet, the baby will be a stutterer.

If you see a yellow boxcar on a train going by, close your eyes and don't look at the rest of the train or it would be bad luck.

If a bird flies in your house, there will be a death in the family.

If you are talking to or about someone and call them by another persons name, that other person is talking about you.

When squirrels build nests low in trees, it's going to be a cold winter.

Singing in bed will cause you to wake up crying.

If a praying mantis spits in your eye, you go blind.

Playing with matches or fire causes bed wetting.

If you sweep or mop under a young girl's feet, she will never marry.

If you sleep with a dish rag under your pillow, you will be married within a year.

If you pull one gray hair out of your head, 7 will take it's place.

If one dreams of a death, there will be a birth. (Presumably short time span).

If one dreams of a birth, there will be a death.
(Presumably short time span).

Ringing sound in the ear means a death of someone you know.

Do not walk with a blind person's cane, for you will surely go blind.

If you lie, a bump will appear on your tongue. (Lie Bump).

Dreaming the same thing over again three times will make it come true.

Some people say there is no such thing as luck. Whether you believe in luck and superstition or not, I hope you have enjoyed your time spent with Granny.

www.ingramcontent.com/pod-product-compliance
Ingram Content Group UK Ltd.
Pitfield, Milton Keynes, MK11 3LW, UK
UKHW041836200726
13854UKWH00003BA/1166